Walking the Marches

Sam Burnside

Acknowledgements are due to the following publications in which some of these poems first appeared:
Ambit; Visions (USA); Honest Ulsterman; Salmon;
New Irish Writing (Irish Press); Quarto; New Irish Writing (Sunday Tribune); New Writing from Ireland; The Irish Review; The Glynns; Poets Aloud, 1988; Poetry Ireland; BBC Northern Ireland; Borderlines; Riverine; Derry Journal; Foyle Civic Trust Journal; Ulster Tatler; BBC Radio Foyle; Gown; Irish Labour History Society News; Larkin Society Journal; The Great Book of Clashganna; Donegal Democrat; Fortnight; Cyphers; Living Landscape Anthology.

Cover Artwork by David Hill.
Typesetting and design by Johan Hofsteenge.
Printed by Colour Books Ltd., Dublin.
Hardcover Binding by Kenny's Fine Binding, Galway.

The publisher acknowledges the financial assistance of the Arts Council of Northern Ireland in the publication of this volume.

© Sam Burnside, 1990. All rights reserved.
ISBN 0 948339 41 1 hardcover £8.00
ISBN 0 948339 42 X softcover £4.95

Salmon Publishing
Auburn, Upper Fairhill, Galway, Ireland.

Contents

Outside the City	1
Anamnesis	4
Walking the Marches	6
Easter Island	7
Inheriting the Earth	8
Six Loughs	9
Scenes from an Irish Calendar	11
A Crude Cabin in Mayo	14
Light	15
Foyle	17
Her Recipe	18
James Hope	19
In The King's Head, London	21
Evil's Face	22
Paddling in Down	23
Marble Arch Caves	24
A Hard Frost	25
Belfast	27
The Day the Russian Circus came to Creggan Roundabout	28
Her Farmyard	30
In Memory of John Hewitt	32
In and Out of Derry	33
Silence	34
Cultivation	35
An Irish Sacrament	36
Soldiers	37
Walking to School	38
A New Painting on an Irish Wall	39
April, 1980	41
Untitled	42
Mary Ann McCracken	43

Eleventh Night 45
Orangemen 46
Sonnet for a One-Legged Sailor 47
Born Circa 75 A.D. 48
Weeding 51
Murder Mile Road 53
THE GRAND TOUR 55
   Van Gogh in the Glens 55
   Leonardo on Rathlin 56
   Hogarth on Cavehill 57
   Pieter Breughel Wintering in Ulster 58
   Michaelangelo on Stand-by 59
THE ULSTER WAY 61
   Prologue 63
   The New Bridge, Londonderry - Travelling East 65
   Castlerock 66
   Passing a Flax Mill 67
   Coleraine Square 68
   Passing Church Gates 70
   Island Magee Inheritance 71
   Beyond Cavehill 72
   A Disused Hill Quarry 73
   The Sperrins 74
   A Hospital on the Outskirts of a Town 75
   One Face in a Dancehall 76
   A Masked Ball in the Big House 77
   University Libraries 78
   Country Towns 79
   Graveyards 80
   From Grainan of Aileach to Derry - 21 December 81
   Epilogue 82

Outside the City

Upon leaving the city
Proceed Northwards till you come to Fanny Wylie's Bridge
Keep Straight on (passing two lots of standing stones)
Before turning Westwards towards Rocky Hill. Go through Grania's
Gap, cutting in between Eskaheen and Scalp Mountains;
There you will find yourself on the high ground
Between Swilly and Foyle.

First, I saw your feet were heavy. The incessant rain
Must have lodged, cuckoo-like, inside you body,
In your lower limbs, its atomic weight visible in the curve
Of your mouth. Your lips dipped with each step you took.
Each mimed, music-hall gesture appeared hilarious, at first.
Then the clouds lifted and I saw Bedlam in your eyes,
Alive and well inside your head.

Now look about you
At steep Scalp Mountain
At gentle Eskaheen
To your left, see
Where the Children of Lir lived, according to legend.
Turning Westwards, notice the fine sweeping course
Taken by the Lough.
Observe the Russian factory ships lying low in the water
In the lee of Inch Island. Vikings may have used Swilly,
As an entrance, once or twice;
We do not know, for a certainty.

Up here the look on your face changes
As the climate inside your head changes.
I am lightning and thunder, you say
Electrical storm
Swim and swirl about your skull,
You want autonomy, you say.
You think that is being alone,
Moated,
As you were until I ventured along.
But then, I was always there, you say, waiting.

The people farm a little; they fish a little;
They have a little dole from Dublin.
The land is poor in places;
Marshy, yes, but there may be oil under it,
And the coastline is rich in wrecks
(It is said some contain gold.)
And tomorrow a deal may be carried off.
It all depends on who you know.
And the people have faith.
And it is so peaceful here; so restful; and the air is so healthy.

They explained that some would look to your mother or your father,
That others believe an understanding of environment can provide clues;
And some put their faith in getting the chemical balance right.
Some find enlightenment contained in myth
(Mother means death, which sounds rather unreal)
While others engage in talk, talk, talk. In the pub, just now,
When we sought refuge from the elements,
I noticed how your brow was patinated with fine snowflakes
And how you studied the presence.

Feel free to walk about, as you will. The taking
Of photographs is encouraged. And a branch of heather
Bloom will make a pleasing token of remembrance
When dried.

It was when they were singing and playing
And calling for more and more drinks
That I saw the pain in you; your stare to the wall,
The twist and turn of your fine fingers.
The mist had come down. The tide was running to full.
The rock you stood on shrunk small.
It is me, and what I am to you, you say.
I am a storm brewing, I am a shark waiting, you say.

Descend through the wide glen.
Circumnavigate the standing stone at Ashdevlin.
Then, before returning to the city,
Walk along the shore as far as Fahan, place of poets and saints.
On a night when the tide has retreated far
You may be graced to hear men's buoyant voices singing devotions.
On a clear night you may be lucky enough to see Abbey walls
Raised again
Standing white between water and mountain.

Anamnesis

A woman I know, in a dream watched her daughter
Lift out coolly, between finger and thumb, her eyes
And dance, delightedly, in dark danger,
Refusing to face the fear age would have taught.

They, they are fond of calling her The Old Mother:
Strange, how so fertile a land
(Salmon, trout, deer there on the rising slopes,
Clutters of birds)
Should misconceive so often.

Possessing no natural minerals, no noble metal,
They made themselves a metaphysical wealth:
Found Fool's Gold, and concocted a dull-
Plated thing, hollow-hearted, now long tarnished.
They touched then the paradox of blood, life-giving
When contained, staining eternally when splashed.

We, we were the foster-sons;
Strange in the place for years, but
(Building, pragmatically fencing,
Delving fore-arms into the earth)
Turned husbandman and midwife by necessity,
Quickening a slow, old unnatural one.

Grope, grope, all, for the twisted rope of memory,
Stroke the ragged ends for that familiar fibre;
Finding, discarding, fumbling, finally stumbling
Out into the place that is the present,

Unsure if that hangman, history, pulled the lever,
Or if we ourselves, daily, commit communal suicide:
As if some race-memory (lemming-like) fools our sense
Of distance. A view of reality must be long-sighted,

Or leap of faith may be fool's jump. Ha, two fools together,
But can we, with bent heads and fingers stiff trace back
(Through the warped mythology,
Beneath the heaped earthworks),
Till we find title-deeds to this soil, establish
Rights-of-way through these pre-Celtic northlands.

Walking the Marches

There is no peace to be had
With all these comings and goings;
The guttering messages
Are sent by every root and branch
Beneath your feet through veined rock
And the worm-ploughed, rising land:
So, you need to walk the marches
Daily; to test with thumb and eye
The fastenings of gate, stake and fence.
Picnickers; preachers; poachers.
You find them under your hedges,
Shirt-collars undone, wrecks of meals
Scattered across the sward,
The soles of their boots upturned
Anonymously.
Lately, even the half-set sun
Wickedly trespasses through
The thickest of old blackthorn,
Blindingly.

Easter Island
For Bill
And David, Who Came Later

Innishcoo when we arrived
Was wind-storm bound,
All night long it blew, then came morning
Soft, with larks, seabirds and swans
Who, your wife said, were heading
North to love in Greenland,
Honking overhead while we
Walked the island, passing over
At low tide seeking if neighbours
Were to be found elsewhere, but
The low white shells, thatched or slated,
It made no difference, were empty.
One we found was full of bones,
Sheep or cow, we were not qualified
To say which. Then darkness fell
And the storm rose once again
Troubling the bays and inlets,
Ruffling the late moon, bothering
Through window sash our thin drapes
Until the morning's light calmed
Them and the embracing waters.
Then, when it was all ended,
We crossed over the narrow sea
And drove across Donegal:
We passed over the border
From one country to another
And had to stop and answer questions,
Where were we coming from?
Where were we going to?

Inheriting the Earth

Like a ratchet, the sound of the buzz saw
Draws us closer to where they have fallen:
Like Samsons sheared at the knees,
These summer evening lovers lie
In sweet-scented greenery; they embrace,
For the first time, their own long shadows;
Each dry, flat stump a disappointment
Inserted between desire and consummation.

The words come tumbling after. The leather-
Booted protesters trample the weed, Love-
lies-a-bleeding. Planners and protesters
Locked in dispute can make nothing of it.
Across the grass the saw sings. Each trunk, seduced
In turn by the blade, sprays out dry wood-chips.

Six Loughs

No bird sings on Belfast Lough.
On Carlingford, on Swilly, on Foyle
Silence has settled, like death in a house
Long prepared. Tall rushes, like mourners
Standing in rain, shadow the waters
Of the two Ernes.

After all the fraudulent mouthings
That for so long revised the truths
All our people saw and knew, this is rest.
She consorted with the other sort; his behaviour
Was anti-social; this one was an informer;
We will not tolerate

Criminal elements. In the meantime
On some bare headland there stands a grey-cloaked figure
Still, bell in hand, eying grey swans, waiting
For another Patrick. But we need a long silence
Now; and a good rain-shower to wash away this sense
That words may mean anything.

So, the place must lie fallow,
While wind-storm and rain-cloud curve
In round the Mournes and over the Sperrins,
From the West crossing the Bluestack mountains
To bleach skeletons, to achieve time's ends
On bodies buried with lies

And false justifications, spoken over them,
After the beatings and the hoodings and the shootings
By roadside and and by lake and by mountain stream,
In fields of grass and grain stained twice:
Who now could celebrate the miller's loaves
Bequeathed to us.

On Slemish and in Armagh silence reigns.
A silence carried up from deep Newgrange inhabits
Antrim's glens. The very air is thick with it
And bird and beast wait for some ending of it,
For the breaking of it by some fresh word.

Scenes from an Irish Calender

Pubs

i.
Caught, confabulating across
Pints of black stout
Capped and hatted, indoors as out,
Their faces harrowed by elements of time,
You want to draw closer, to listen to them,
To the warm, plain, dark secrets
They polish, like Socrates, into words.

ii.
In the background, melting into shadow,
Thoughtful, pensive, sober, the women.

Stone Cross

Rising out of a green, cropped lawn
The burnished, bronzed stone tilts
Bleached where there is
No landscape for background
No figure for foreground.
The crossed arm depleted hugely at one corner:
The wrinkled pattern is bitten into, for ever.

Rocks

Rocks, grey as seals' backs
Pitted by time
Their tonguelessness
   seeks our attention
Would preach to us
   of what we already know
The presence, the scope, the weight,
The density of time's eternity.

Georgian Doors

All be-stepped; be-decked with brass
Furniture the sun might leave warm
For the night-palm of your hand.
Panelled well and well shelled
In reds and blues and greens;
Crowned with the lightest touch,
A fanning brilliance.

Thatch

The yellow thatch hides mice
And sucks down the sun
Out of the bluest sky
You could ever imagine;
The driver and his donkey
Pass
Eyes to the front
His cigarette droops
The reins curve and hang, the
Long, thin stick shivers
Anenst one grey flank;
A black-trousered leg trails
Over the edge of eternity.

Governance

Away across a strand
The pony trots full circle
Again and again and again.
The lunging-rein lengthens and shortens.
The beach, the sea and sky take breath.
The man has no hurry on him;
The long suck of the tide deflates time.
He turns and turns and turns
Head, neck, hoof, eye and hand,
Sand-grain, sea-wind and sea-splash
Turning full-circle
Again and again and again.

A Crude Cabin in Mayo

A flat hand
Sweeps and wipes
The mist that masks
Like a modesty cloth
The empty night.

Underneath rain,
Faces in the window
By cancerous water
Drops and cells
Are eaten black.

In curling seas
Dolphins speed on.
Across the Burren
Lichens inch outwards.
We are weather-bound.

Light

i.
A child's hand reaches out to touch a peach
Her fingertips tingle in anticipation,
The globulous clinging dew's on the skin
Of the fruit on the canvas; it enters her head:
Mind-fingers mark her white summer dress, and then
Her eyes clear and she smiles, feeling foolish.

ii.
The landscape is there, it shall speak for itself:
It will seduce eyes, while the leases run out,
While men cart fools' gold down from the mountains,
Or trudge, season after season, to the sunken graves
Of those who in the darkness of dream ask us
To weep over their emptying constructions.

iii.
They are lessons in magnanimity
The clouds and the hills; look down the Swilly
At layered peaks, washed this day and the next
With every bog-colour art can mix,
Or into the Mournes, composed and new-cleaned,
Tucked up beneath blankets of egg-white whipped.

iv.
There is nothing exclusive about the climate,
About the ballet of cloud and sun on the hillsides,
Or about the way rock and valley guides rivers,
Or in the sun, cliff and air's lifting and tossing
Of composed birds. It is more than just ceremony,
Less than marriage, this over-looked courtship.

v.
The light on Ulster keeps changing;
It reforms radically the landscape;
It taunts decorous, slothful painters
Who would keep the conventions alive
Setting a varnished bloom on canvas
That will neither rot nor yield its seed.

Foyle

Far out, on the west bank, petrified trees
Cling to the steep flanks of the River Foyle;
They were mere saplings when deep tenders took
The dark-clothed men and inaccessible women
Down past the sand ridges to the waiting ships.
Age, and the insistent wind from the east,
Has crooked all their limbs: they squat, crippled,
Denuded, on the brae faces, their deep-digging roots
Wringing life from the land, tippling greedily; offering,
Among that netted web, no asylum for their betrayed seeds
That must drift on the wind to flourish God knows where.

Her Recipe
For Mary, Myra, Sive and Cathy

A dish for salt,
A dish for oil,
Two candles; a black cross
And a white cloth;

She had them all to hand;
All the linens for her purpose
Laid aside on her wedding day
(She prayed all their life together for his happy death)
A readiness for the ritual that would cleanse her of grief
So successful that the death touch, the cold death kiss,
Had been practised, and practised, until perfected.

She brought the children in
And she told them. She brought them in
To the cold hand: she put their
Fingers to the flesh: touch now and you will never
Fear death.

She could not see herself
Through the white shrouds;
And the smell of what was left of him
She buried under other smells.

A white cloth;
A black cross; two candles;
A dish of oil;
A dish of salt;

Her catalogue,
Her recipe.

James Hope

i

*"Discourage the linen trade and you will have
soldiers."* Lord Hillsborough

You should have acquired and used the jaw-bone
Of an ass! But no, you were too decent
A man to go in for that tit-for-tat
Old Testament stuff.
Too intelligent
To believe in the power of might over evil.

You should have forged and used a good, steel sword;
You could have left the land clean for your sons
(You had no daughter)
Ready for seeding
Ready for a new breed as hungry
For truth, learning and liberty as you.

You should have built a towering guillotine
Hired ancient females
To hunker under
It, malicious and dribbling over red
Heads whorling under sunlight and shadows:

More power to you, you turned your back on that solution.

ii

"*With God all things are possible.*" James Hope

Jemmy Hope: weaver; Presbyterian;
Man of no property; fifteen-weeks schooled;
One of nature's nobility, Madden
Said of him, of him who hated love of rank,
Who wanted democracy to tingle
At peoples' fingertips, as finely balanced
As one of his looms, with justice singing
Like a shuttle across Ireland's warp and weft.

You used words like dignity and temperance;
You spoke of the virtues of fortitude
And forbearance; you wrote of pensioned
Clergy, instigating hate, for conscience sake,
Bought magistrates, fat gentry, and those whose lust
For wealth made them cattle-herds over others.

What you wanted, and died with faith in, was a clean revolution.

In The King's Head, London

Through the open door, under the street lights,
The screen-familiar bulk of a London taxi
Flows quietly past. In the raucous King's Head
A red-haired woman of fifty dances wild
Jigs on the partly-wooded floor. Suspicious,
Always, of the black brew found anywhere
But Dublin town we ask a knowing man:
"Ah," he says, "Ye'd better stick to the beer."
He has the low, clear speech of West Ireland
That carries cleanly through the rough-edged din
Of fiddle and feet. Like Christian slaves, back
To Rome we carry our ritual, our white-headed God,
Over the Irish Sea to this autocratic house
With its space-war machines, its mild and its bitter.

Evil's Face

That man I met and sat down with
Saying words over the meat and the drink
And moving us to touch hand to hand
Conjuring up as part of his grace
The memory of parted children;
In ranging conversation he named
Evil's presence, "It can come",
He said, "into any room,
Like smoke creeping under the door."
"It may not be a thing, like that,"
I whispered, distant from conviction,
"It may be a human part of us
Like love or hate or fear or pity."
"No," he said, "evil has a face."

I could catalogue the places where it was
Up and down the country
If I wished; I do not know, nor do I care,
What its form is but only that
Where it is a man or woman always is
And they all together with a victim.

Paddling in Down
Newry, June 20 1990

I found myself
Standing outside
The Frontier Cinema.
Like Sweeney
Before me
I fled in-
Land, North-
Wards,
The Mournes
Billowing
Around my ankles.

Crossmaglen
Shut, shell-like,
Artfully
Closed and definite,
Shone in the sun,
Briefly, and was gone.

Marble Arch Caves

Images of a cave maintain themselves clearly
And cleanly in my mind. They were there long before
I ventured underground. I knew about the hole;
The descent; the zero light; the architecture
Whose arches carry the earth's erratic burden;
I never conceived the centre of the world so sodden.
I had no regard for the secrets of rivers,
Their persistence, how they finger their ways through rocks
In silence and secrecy, kissing the seeking
Lips of blind fish, insinuating their designs
Upon the graveled floors of dark cathedrals,
Conveying the caressed massed threads of white worms.
Up above, some dreaming men squint astride hayricks
Hoarsely whispering love down the night-sights of fire-sticks.

A Hard Frost

God, but it was great
To be up and out
And it a morning singing
With icicles popping off gates
And on the line clothes
Left out wringing wet
Grown stiff as boards
Flat and still
And all furred with the white
Frost that would cling
To the very insides of your mouth
If you left it open.

> *Take that wee hand-axe and go out and break the ice*
> *On the big water-trough and let the horse get a drink.*
> *And don't slip and fall on that axe!*
> *And mind, don't use the sharp edge, or it'll skite up*
> *And hit you on the face!*

The trees painted white are sparkling
The air is pin-tipped and tingling
An axe to hand and Robinson Crusoe
And Scott of the Antarctic are remembered
And then forgotten in the face
Of real work to be done.

The ice goes mushy where you hammer it
The sound frightens the horse into a gallop
His hooves make the ground
Tremble like the skin of a beaten drum
Yellow water seeps up through the bobbing bits
And there is the danger
Of being splashed. The ice-sheet gives
Eventually. There could have been
Good sliding here, but you find
At nine
That your fast breath quickly clouds the issue.

Belfast

Past Cavehill, breathless, night-capped still in cloud,
Belfast, shrouded in early-morning mist
Lies astride the Lagan. On runs the road;
Descending from the high Antrim brightness
Down into a place of ships and sea, crane
And high-rise flats: down into a dead light
That will linger awhile yet but will lift
Before shrill voices call the first edition.
An awkward, irascible city, full,
Past the brim, of brash bickering and full
Too of compassion and a hard charity.
It's had its Tories and its Whigs, its brief-
Lived Radicals and its too-few Liberals.
Her mute giants stand, feet entombed in concrete.

The Day the Russian Circus came to Creggan Roundabout

An old elephant
Chains on two trunked ankles
Turned a cold eye
On me and my pupils
As it passed
It blew into my ear
"I forget nothing".

The girl on the trapeze
Swung and swung and swung
And swung magnetically over our heads
And the heads of the others opposite
She was only young too and tonight
Her hand and eye
Were out of kink

Somehow and she missed
The outstretched arms
Of the swallowing white catcher.
Three times she fell
Into the ballooning net below before
A swell of hissing sent her off
Running, stiff-armed and tiny, for cover.

Condemned by her calling
To repeat the same mistake
She appeared later to fall
And be tossed by the net
Up through a last rainbow of tears.
We left then, to be followed
At a distance judged discreet

By the classes from the Catholic school.
We stopped to look at the oldest elephant
Chained in the canvas tunnel to a small peg;
Her cold old-maidish eye gave no sign
Nor asked for pity. She blew across my ear
As I passed under staggering lights,
"I forget nothing".

Her Farmyard

Twenty times or more a day
She would cross over the cobble-stone-paved yard
From the cusp of their house to the swimming midden
To slop out the sodden potato skins and tea leaves.
Bits of egg shells, pared cores of cooking apples
Pitched and sown across the cow-dung mound,
Steaming on frosty mornings when the air stung.
Her empty-eyed boots passing over trapped, cobwebby ice,
Stuff that drank the winter sun where it dared
Flirt and flit in the depths of cobbled sumps.
Each one of her decades there had contained
Dogs: always two animals whose slinking, narrow shapes
Criss-crossing the hills and meadows like cloud-
Shadows marshalled the drifting flocks before appearing
In the yard, one to wag and fawn: the other
Always was a whiner, whinging day and night,
Set off by sun or moon, or anything
Beyond its empty reach; its lean brother
Never off the go, ratting, seldom sleeping.
There was little truck between these two parties,
Except when sent out there with one purpose, then
They were unctuous in their convoluted meshwork,
Doctrinaire in their domination of schism
Among their flocks but, still, factioneers themselves.
It was here that countless summer evenings had found her
Stepping through the warmth of bee-sound, through the rumbling
Peace of cows in the byre, the strib of milk
Drawn down by her husband's hands, striking bucket's solid bottom,
Stitching in her mind the smells to the sounds
To the tastes of her life. Blessed by low swallows,
But never by her own rough hand, mountained and valleyed

And hardened with age, not a hand for smoothing fur
But given to the penance of living here;
A beautiful, magnificent non-icon
That crabbed hand, rising and falling in sympathy out here
As she walks alone, with those jaundiced two combing
The darkening hills, containing splinter groups
Bringing back to the bunching clique breakaways,
Forming coteries in the lea of wattle fences
Plaited and interlaced and gridded
As soundly as nets for butterflies; still, underfoot
She senses the stretching, yearning ice that ribs
And interlaces this her own ground, even in August.

In Memory of John Hewitt

Purity of line is everything;
George Herbert knew it, and John Donne
Too talked about the bounding outline,
That distinction precisely inserted
Between reality and Art:
As pure as the published blood line of the Gael
Or the perfect border planters dug across the land.

Purity of anything becomes totalitarian, eventually.

John Hewitt was aware of that.
He conceived himself to be a citizen
Of a world wide in time and space,
Though as one who happened importantly to live here
He felt the value of place,
The worth of light, clay and cloud:
But in solemn talk it was the names of men
   (John Toland; William Morris; James Hope;
    Henry Joy McCracken and Cobbett and William Drennan),
Names that turned again and again on his deliberate tongue
In a catalogue of dissent against injustice;
His telling
A testament to Diggers and Levellers and Chartists.

He spent his days working among images created by others
And his evenings handling words of his own choosing.
He was a maker, not of artifacts or flim-flams,
But of poems that stand like plain, deal tables,
Part measured against part, joints smoothed for ease of use;
A maker of poems whose meanings stand isolated from chance
By his sense of where in the world the centre of gravity is.

That honest sense stands between him and his countrymen
Whose words ranted and rant up from bellies hard with hate.

In and Out of Derry

The Donegal mountains, sitting out there
Blue, blunt heaps of lignite, sad hinterland
To a burning city; and the heavy stone walls
And houses, shops and factories, fronts erased,
Sag into the bog-ground while light title-deeds
Change hands in the silent communion of commerce.
The city's odd shop-keepers, sour and mean enough,
Clang their rat-trap tills and keep the doors guarded.
For there are those who disregard limb and life
Who blast and bomb with red-eyed, mad-dog malice;
Then again there are those who disregard even that,
Who live only for profit and tomorrow's gain.
If things were different there'd be no buts but
Life goes on, has, and somehow always will,
Despite the bombs and assassinations.
We are successful in ignoring these things,
And carry on, forming - from the old twin cultures -
Some new kind of human resistance and bloody-minded calmness.
In a hundred years it will warrant a paragraph
In some history book: the common people they'll call us,
(Our fathers, they'll note, paid a shilling for a rat,
And ate quartered dogs to live), and they'll not know
Or not reckon the fear in pubs, in shops,
The daily bumping over ramps, the body-searches,
The tension of fire-sirens singing in darkness.

Silence

When my dry dust
   scattered at evening time
   by blindly flung hand
   and arm stiff with rage and despair,
   settles on cool water,
   the final coming together
   will be hidden
   if calmness is lost.

All shall be lost,
   for time eats all
   documentation of public memory,
   and monuments to private witness
   must marry with obscurity,
   like a voice swallowed by a storm
   whose rising and ending is purpose,
   or no purpose.

Cultivation

The snuffle of each new one
Fighting out from between
A pair of guiding hands
Dunting up to the udder
Of the grunting mother:
She, her wind-sock of a body
Without a single flop
Shovelled and shrugged and jellied
Into accommodation,
Lifts and turns her head
With each new attachment,
Only her eyes, under swinging
Lamp, wild and electric. Then,
After sound, sight: the pinkness,
A dry, straw-chaffed, salmon-ness,
Mild after the hard, red
Blood-issue from the ritual
Cutting and the tying
Of the eel-like life-cord,
Skin, not-textured but young,
Against strewn straw, harsh and yellow,
Rippling under grasping lamp-light.
Darkness wrapping around
That happening with its body-heats
Its ancient murmerings
Its swelling waves of smells
Its treasury of golds:
The night thundering around old and new life,
Cloaking the husbandman and the midwife.

An Irish Sacrament
27 June 1986

Come, stand beside me under this great dome;
On one side those who gave birth and nurtured
You, and on this my parents and brothers.
Let the long flow of life that brought us here
Ebb for an instant; let us then unite,
Together, urging life forward again,
Being part of it, and to be it
For always, or as long as we want to.
Eschew narrow places with God put on a plate,
Us and Him roofed in, an official
Legislating each to each; that is, at best,
An odd view of love, a queer engagement:
The ring of our two hands coming together
In the pious drill that knows no earthly end.

Soldiers

What is it they go back to
When they go back east from here:
There's the pies with mushy peas
In Doncaster, Hull and Leeds,
And sons, cousins and nephews
With their own black and white wars
Being educated for the dole while
Waiting to be told stories about us
Here: white faces seen behind rain
Through the peep holes of saracens:
On an intimacy not
Much greater than that we're known
Far and near.

Thin teachers with wire glasses,
Indiscriminately named
Paddy by their scouse classes,
Carting two big volumes of Proust
On their camping trip to France,
Then Yeats on the Liverpool ferry
To feel his own weight on their lips
As the lights of Belfast blink
Out of another dark night,
Coming home for a week's talk;
Answering, its not great, really,
But what is there for us here
Only unemployment.

Walking to School

Walking to school one way and home another
On one side a shugh, a ditch on the other:
Of four miles, after a day's wrestling with English Kings,
The last two were the slow-footed, soft ones
Past a fairy-thorn patched faithfully with tinker's rags,
Or harvesting Easter's molten yellow
Whin blossom to mark on the fertile symbols
Before smashing to eat the mute life out of them.
Over bogs, moors, whins; through gorse and golden bracken
Coursed by roads and lanes and boreens and tracks
And pads; past lake and lough; through glen and valley
With lovely Deirdre and Bonnie Prince Charlie
And Bruce and his spider and Welsh dragons unslain
Vying for space with Robin Hood and Cuchulainn.

A New Painting on an Irish Wall

i
The riffs and ruffs of my breath
Burst between me and the stone.
The valley below was full
Of running, river water;
In places there may have been sheet ice,
I am sure I heard it disintegrate.
My naked, warm hand drew closer
To the stone, as if opposites
Do attract. The stigmata
Of Irish history fresh enough
To cause a misty imprint
On the innocence of a soft, pink palm.
Below, the crisp sound of glass splintering
Sang through the winter-morning calm.

ii
Under the arched gateway
Where the footpath narrows
Stand on the narrow ground
Where street lights fail
To reach. If you are brave
Enough to wait quietly
To listen properly
You will hear the sounds
Of horses passing.
Let your hand stroke stone. Listen well,
Out of darkness, under the perfect arch,
To the simple rattle and spark of those
Iron-clad wheels turning on old stone,
To the song of lash slicing through to bone.

iii
At one place, the mish-mash
Of brick-work and stone-work
(Its builders' hands long loosened in dust)
Rough-cast, pebble-dashed, white-washed
Holds close to its tone and texture
One short, weak lick of sunlight
Squeezing in between western showers.
Stand up close and see
How edges of messages
Wobble over the heaving texture,
How word, image and symbol
Ride their layered foundations.
Here you will find only answers.
Such ground is not yet fit for questions.

iv
Another night falls and the solitary
Inventor comes with aerosol in hand
Prepared to blanket the softness that time
Has achieved on plaster, brick and stone.
Ten thousand voices guide his quick hand;
In all honesty he cannot sign his name:
He is a medium, not a Blavatsky
Or anything like her, just a medium.
Out on the river a coal boat lies-to
Holding blackness in its guts, waiting
For morning to lift the darkness that falls
As soft as duck down over stern and bow.
On the hill it is finished. He turns away
His face obscure in shadow, his heart tight-swathed.

April, 1980

Stormont has been filleted. Ironically,
The meat, the flesh, the blood has gone,
Puritanically taken away; only the bones
Remain, washed daily in soft Ulster rain.
And we circling in low over it:
Cheap-rate shuttlers who today blandly gaze
Down on what we never owned or entered,
Although it was ours, symbol of our place
Patch-worked still, green and cool after London,
Texture and line of home. But those white bones,
That hard shell, what echoes resound in it?
Does 'Not an Inch' tremble from wall to wall,
Locked mockingly in that white, marble-like,
Bright, clean, strong-walled structure we had faith in.

Untitled

Living alone in a low hut,
My valley, little more than a shugh,
Damp and bog-bottomed,
Dominated by two rounded hills
Each height nippled
By Academy and Cathedral,
My days and nights worried
By figures travelling constantly
Between the two horizons.

My feet on the marsh have trodden in
Blades of grass; stepping, however neatly,
Between my door and the well I have left
My sign. The dull sound
Of bones beneath robes is another.

Mary Ann McCracken
*"She has bequeathed to her birthplace
a legacy of unusual nobility and courage."*

From one light to the next was as far
As the eye could see. Up Rosemary Street,
Down High Street, in and out of the Shambles,
Through mud and horse-dung half a foot deep, wains
And dogs and strolling officers mingling;
Elizabeth Fry and Mary Wollenstoncroft
Raised on up-turned wooden buckets, signalling
With candles; the Northern Star hoisted up
Like a rickety Chinese kite, all glue
And string, its tail of old rags trailing
Down through wafting speeches, spring-breezes of words,
Drizzles of opinion, a hail-storm of ideas;
Ships' Captains and winds blowing in from France
Bringing the seeds of three flowers westwards
Before taking them up to be carried again
Westwards, to be broadcast across prairie and plain.

Most nights a knock would bring her to the door
Another old man, hungry and cold, begging;
As like as not the heel prints of small-pox
Irregular on his face; destitution
Inscribed on the skin of his opened palm;
His tongue lying limp between tightened jaws;
His tongue lying idle between his gums;
A bit of bread the only thing on his mind.

She lived in a place and at a time
And among men and with women whose minds
Were steady and inflexible and, she
Claimed, invulnerable to any weapon
But reason. They denied slavery's profit;
Rebelled, not in dark places, but openly,
Spelling out in black and white their just abhorrence
At what caused black John Moore to run away
From that house in Princess Street where he had been
Installed: "We will not only harbour him,
But will enable him, by pecuniary donations,
To carry on legal prosecution
Against his intended enslaver".
Her friend Russell refusing cake decorated
With slave-sugar from the West Indies
Leaves on this side of the grave that image;
Straight-backed in the year 1860
An old woman 17 days off 89
Believing in the power of straight-tongued reason
She distributes anti-slavery leaflets
Below the gang-plank, hoping to save America,
By now "the land of the tyrant and the slave",
Sends off emigrants briefed to speak about justice.

Talk about chickens coming home to roost:
Cock-sure, now, they're sending the leaflets back.
Laundered by the wash of two hundred year's
Wear and tear; her fingerprints are erased;
A new title page has been prepared and appended:
Copyright claimed; there is nothing new under the sun.

Eleventh Night

Then, there was a bonfire on every height
Splattering the night skies with scarlet;
There were fifes, there were drums, there were boys on old
Bikes without headlamp or tail-light or bell or brake,
Careless on this one night of the tall, silent peelers.
Little, thin-faced men up alleys passing bottles in sly kinship
And strong farmers, standing dimly in work-stained, dirt-stiff boots
Backs to the wall, turned corner-boys for just the hour
Spitting and accepting fags from fast lads eager to be men.
Sparks fly high from root and branch, and smoke belches from bald
                                                                                     old tyres
There's a hiss in the air and a surge in their hearts and a crazy
Call to abandon as blood-wet wrists dance on the skins of the big
                                                                                              Lambegs.

Orangeman

No duncher today.
Sedately he marches in time
Amid the solemn mass
Of the black bowler-hatted;
Head jugged in stiffened felt:
As obscene somehow as the loin-clout
And guilt
Dry missionaries
Once pinned on the hips of savages.

Sonnet for a One-Legged Sailor

His father, who was one-legged also,
Walked on a limb he had carved from a tree
Using his strong right arm and a sharp knife.
This man rests his weight on a thing of tin,
Supplied and fitted by the Welfare State.
He sends it once a year to be serviced,
And hopes, one day, to have it microchipped,
Rather like the guided missile that one day found him.
Rendered faithful in this way he displays
None of the passion his old father had
When he made the wood chips fly in the air;
Missing a leg, but carving his own parts,
Shrewdly making one of oak and one of pine,
In his own time and to his own design.

Born Circa 75 A.D.
A Lough Neagh sequence

i
In the first century after Christ lived,
In a green field or out of a flat rock,
A fountain of pure, clear water that lifted
Towards heaven, was drowned in its own flood.
Blind waters topped their confinement
And groped towards the plains of five counties;
Kissed the turf, sod, clod and meadow-clay of
Antrim and Down and Armagh and Tyrone,
Caressed to sleep a low plain of Derry.
Ram's Island rose and on it rose a tower,
Coney Island rose and drew to its shore
A saint. Carved stone cross and capstoned Dolmen
And tower house with bawn and fine, walled graveyard
Stand by the countless, silent sleepers all.

ii
How many million cubic gallons
Settled into a smooth sheet of liquid crystals
Arranged, shorn and rolled mirror smooth!
She sends out at sunrise her sleepy giants;
Her children; they love to watch their shadows
Settling on the stretching, yearning surface;
They love to dream of times long ago,
To make fond wishes for the days ahead.
The deep water of Lough Neagh, it is said,
Has power to petrify any living thing
Be it body of man or beast, or image
Of face. Only the flat-jawed, boneless eel
Coming and going, coming and going,
Thrives there in the black glair of Balor's eye.

iii
When John Carey built his Temple of Liberty,
Learning and Select Amusements at Toome,
Victoria reigned; her Empire has fallen; he
Lies in Duneane Churchyard, his Temple forgotten,
The walls as flat as St. Toide's church on Lough Beg,
As low as Salter's Castle or O'Connor's Stronghold
Now mere ribbed earthworks on the far shores of Lough Neagh
Each attended only by dark and silent shadows.
The Holy well lying inland from the Three Isles
Rises clear and cool, just as it did when the place
About it, in the magical act of naming,
Was whispered over by someone who tongued it
The Plain of the Wood of Wild Garlic. Church Island
Lies bare in Lough Beg; names are title-deeds.

iv
A silver dish, a big cisheen of fish
Scaled blue-grey, a centre-piece decorated
By Castle and Keep, by Church and Round Tower
Holy Well and Wishing Tree, Planter's House
And strong Bawn, Abbey and rising green mound
High Cross, Cairn and Cyst, and always the rivers
Running in and out for the sake of balance,
Through boglands rich in browns and purples.
The sunlight fades: a General burns Antrim
To the ground, flames dancing on the red Lough.
A strange macabre procession of flat figures
Passing by: Henry Joy fleeing Antrim;
A young man hanged on the Bridge of Toome;
They come to sit at Ulster's groaning board.

v

On Friday nights they come from miles around
In rusty old bangers, in nice long Jags;
Taxi-drivers mixing business with pleasure,
Painters and plumbers, male nurses and tic-
Tac men, farmers and computer programmers,
Planter and Gael, but mostly Gael. Tin whistles
Placed carefully in jacket inner pockets
They descend on country pubs, like warriors.
The thing about eel suppers is the drink
Before and the drink after, and the soft
Succulence of long flesh, and the music,
And the madness of men boldly feasting.
Eels cross over; they live on land, in rivers;
The old, secret tongue cannot be severed.

Weeding

I remember being sent out a few times
Long-handled, wooden-jawed thistle-pullers
Resting across my shoulder; it's strange now
The way I notice how then I never heard
The silence in the fields or in the laneways
The way I do now, returning. The very
Air then vibrating with intimate life;
Life was folded in; blackbird and thrush-song
Layered and layered under the green leaves;
Stoat and weasel hidden with fear in ditches;
The length and breadth of the stretched brown acres
Bearded with pin hints of green, the seed-embedded
Germs of life restless and bursting for light
Up through the dusted loam of my groaning fields;
A child's close feet can feel that rush and swelling
While stepping even so lightly the earth.
There was so much there you had to quarter each field,
Set your sights by tree or stone to keep straight
Your line: the other thing to learn was this:
If you want to pull a thistle cleanly
If you want to bring out the whole weed
Without breaking the long thin root, leaving
A legacy of pain for the harvesters,
You must get a firm hold, and you must pull
Straight and steady, straight up without bending
To this side or that, hand and eye in accord,
The power of your whole body forced inwards
Fixed with mind between your two clenched red fists
Between your inward, upward turning wrists
And down through the smooth wooden handles into
The wooden jaws - but mind not to sever

The fibres totally or you will leave
The root intact and ticking deep below
The sleeping seed bed; in dealing with weeds
You soon learn to develop the work-skills
Of tact and balance; the battle instinct
Of when to halt, of when to lay them out
Naked and wet to wither under the sun,
Letting bee-sound and pigeon-sound and wind-
In-seedling-sound bear down heavily upon them.

Murder Mile Road

Murder Mile road
Deployed, uncoils
Like a thin long-length
Infallibly deceptive
Under blue skies, or grey
In rain, sleet or mist, or drowsing
Under bee-sound, under lark-
Song it cannot shake off its name.
Each road-side bog-hole
Each naked tree-form
Throws shadows that cloak
The appellation modest ghosts
Hide within
When the air comes down over Windy Hill
Calling
Caressing the squeamish lips and the earlobes,
The skin, coats, husks and scalps,
The long, thin hair of the trembling dead.

The Grand Tour

Van Gogh in the Glens

What if Van Gogh, already half deaf and pelt bare,
One simmering summer had taken by storm the nine glens
Had stirred the plouting mists lying across Lubitavish and Trostan
Had embraced among fire and flame the crimson thistle
That beards the steep-jawed axe quarries of Cushendun
Had looked past the black, pile-driving wind at buckled oaks
Had fashioned in hot ice the spray forenenst Glenarm.
What if he had lead the headless Shane up Tievebulliagh
Had guided O'Neill fingers across each stone cairn
Had said, *Listen to the shape of it*, had painted
A wind rainbowed with Osian's roar and Hewitt's whisper.
Had he been quickened to rage at the way things are with us
He might yet help unbend us with a bit of passion.

Leonardo On Rathlin

What would da Vinci
Have made of that leg
Knee bent, hooked over nothing
Severed at the ankle-bone
Going nowhere fast
An old stepping-stone
Stood in a caldron
That's boiling up myths
Gory as ten sunsets
Footless and gormless:
He would have dissected
And peeled back
The thick skin, constructed
A foot, and a boot
Engaged the muscles
Somehow, with pulley
And long strong rope looped
Around the Paps of Jura
And that erect rock
At Carrick-a-rede.
With a bit of science
Like that, with a bit
Of art like that, Leonardo
Could have straightened things out.

Hogarth on Cavehill

Hogarth on Cavehill scratching
With conviction on copper
(Red-hot rivets like snowballs flying)
Thin images of villains in the news
For their cruelty with drills
On men, on chairs, centre stage,
Or sitting on a flat stone
Essaying on hedge-school
History-men. *A man is not*
A man till he knocks down
His father and fathers a son;
Ireland's best-loved text stone-laid.

Pieter Breughel Wintering in Ulster

i

Even fifty years ago he could still have felt at home here
Neighbours congregating (men, women and their children)
In farms yards, with dawn just lifting and ice confectioned
Nicely on sagging ash twigs, the wind out surveying for buried nerve
And bone, stepping and fingering the valleys and ridges of set faces;
And then the heavy trudge out over the fields, clay-weighted boots
Anchoring thick-trousered legs and long-skirted legs to the planet.
Even the youngest of them could read the sodden text of turnips
And cabbage and spuds, the gloomy day their theatre and their light.

ii

This year he would still feel at home here; the summer was grand
But now the days grow grey, the landscape is like a big canvas
With many sombre figures in black outline draped above our heads.
Processions and parades and marches, each with its own leader,
Are out foraging and harvesting up and down the city streets
(He would find work here, up cul-de-sacs) their solid bodies all
                                                                encased,
Their heads sheathed in hat and helmet, the heavy eyelids hooded
And their feet humbled by the slurring march imposed. *The purblind
Leading the half-blind.* Breughel could have put a gloss on that.

Michelangelo On Stand-by

In the heady days after ninety-four
The Medici shown the door, Florence shook
And cleared her head, swept out her musty squares,
Ordered spiders out of every corner,
Unbuttoned girdles, exposed her flesh
And heart to the sun, asked Michelangelo
To finger into stone the wild joy in her veins.

i

I wouldn't have the cheek to bring him here:
What would 'forty-two, or 'ninety, or 'sixty-nine
Mean to him who set up that slab, hammered out
And honed in vast defiance David, the once-
Frail slayer of tyrants and bullies
In one season grown fully to selfhood.
The bubbling God-like gift of creation
That in his time mankind found the grasp of;
The separation of light and darkness;
The struggle of the spirit to rise above dust;
His purpose was set on giving wings to
The captive soul, freeing it from matter:
An ecstatic emergence of thigh and forearm
Of torso and gesture from the cold marble
That forms a prison, until aspiration
And hand and eye and heart and human mind
Unite. Our divisions would bore him, I fear.

ii

Although, given that we are like two forms rising
Left shoulder to right shoulder but with feet well
Bedded in black granite, we have emerged enough
To be heated; our heads are half-free and our eyes
Are clear. We want now a hand and wrist released
So as to allow fingertip to meet fingertip.

iii

Yes, given the scope of this place
He could find subjects enough
Men and women here and there
Who stand like David, alone:
And they too have their models:
Humans who perceived the dawn
And sensed the night was ended
And were not afraid to make song
Even though the heavy tribes slept.

The Ulster Way

Prologue

i

Chaucer and Eliot began in April:
Lilacs breeding under showers in a wet,
Bitter fecundity. Two great vehicles
Set rolling through it all: in one a mind
Divorced, reconnoitring the unreal city;
The other, steering straight through a finished place
Where their eyes twinkle in their heads, alright,
As clear as frosty stars in a glass sky.

ii

It is December now, and I've passed through the winter solstice;
The land is bare, frozen and wet, black where morning rain has fallen;
The fire is blazing, and an invitation rests in my hand
Written by a man who once unravelled
For me the threads of Anglo-Irish writings.
Always an after-comer in this country, he has walked the Ulster Way
And has a gentle hankering still to teach and to learn;
Surprised by pious texts on café walls, that we over-see,
Noting carefully, after years of living here, how two fat
Seaside ladies sit together belching in mute company
In the peace and quiet, in the twilight, of a dated eating-house.
Writing, he ended where he began, for the Ulster Way is circuitous.

iii

The flames roar up the chimney
Throwing soot across a sky
Holding promise of mute snow falling.
Underfoot, lies a worked way
Let us follow him along that
Crossing the magic tracks left there by Maeve
On her great march into Ulster
Crossing the sore marks left there by thousands
On their many quick flights to the west.

The New Bridge, Londonderry - Travelling East

The walk, march, shuffle; the flute, fife and pipes.
There is no common ground, only islands.
Stepping over the seabank of one you
Step over into the rest of the world.
The crossing here is three dimensional.
Overhead, the dangerous sky is empty.

Castlerock

From the carpark to the Barmouth
    can take forever
On days when the wind roars and rips
    asunder flocks of birds.
To arrive we have to put our heads down
    and plough on.

Up above, they have re-grouped, easily
    conducting themselves
The wind that shook them apart, if it did,
    gone, and they surfing on.

They always are, and are, and are, and are
    becoming what they are
Never inching back to what or where they were
    but, like rebel angels,
Mounting an airy stairs to their humble province.

Passing a Flax Mill

i

The great water wheel, remorselessly
Crushes all under its paddling palms
Turning it all into a litter of dust -
To dust all returned, abundance heaped high
But uneasily shifting
When the great double doors are thrown open
And the new day's breath licks across the floor.
Meantime, the narrow white river drives on
White-headed and noise-dense and crystallized,
Far from peaty shallows where frog spawn thrives
And its young circle and circle, dizzy,
Like drunkards full on yeasty booze,
Far from the dense deep blue sea.

ii

The flecked sea, that plain of delight,
that rich womb from which speckled salmon leapt
Under the fleet feet of Bran, son of Febal.

Coleraine Square

These street are not all that noisy.
I mind the time when sermons
And even the odd party speech
Promising pie in the sky
Made sane men slip round corners
And in side doors of serene pubs.
Beside, or behind me, footsteps slap,
Feet enclaved in flat gumshoes;
The hand, that voice, the breath
Never far from my skin.
The neon lights flash on
In nuclear discourse
Mouthing, *Big Daddy American Burgers*
And bargains abounding
In every huxter shop.
'*God's spirit will not always strive with man.*'
Stringed Christmas lights sprightly dance
Above the tinsel-clarty streets,
Over the heavy-headed populace
That walks, left-footed or right-footed,
Straddling the brink of light and shade
Where asserted legality stabs:
"*If you die tonight without Christ, My Friend,
Hell will be your due!*"

And from the four corners
Of the square town hall roof
Carols jingle the loose change
In the pockets of late shoppers,
And then her wafting voice drifting,
"Save all your kisses for me . . . "
Dissolving and bending into his,
"Oh, Friend, Sin abounds. Oh, Friend,
Where will You be tonight,
If you should Die? Where, Friend? Oh,
My Friend, you need certainty . . . "

Passing Church Gates

The thin spring sun falls weakly enough,
But by some miracle turns the scaffolding
From rusty function into steel sculpture.
A steeple-jack epicuring up the spire
Inch by far inch, all his worldly needs there
Dangling from a rope fastened to his belt,
Stops, his fingertips read the first rolling
Tremble: a sound of voices enlivens
The afternoon, rising so easily in unison,
And then the great swell of the choir, so strong,
So many ordinary joined; all massed, so;
So restrained, as if they sense the very roof
Might rise before this transformation.

Island Magee Inheritance

They say that the last witch tried in Ireland
    came from this dark townland;
It's a fine place to bring little children
    on a dark, heart-tightening night,
The wind howling round the Gobbins, the sea
    battering the black basalt,
Leaving casual spittle dribbling, white-headed,
    down each blind, furrowed vein.
A fine, queer place to seek a little nook
    of a cave, with its dry shelf
On which to set the heel-end of our candle;
    a fine appropriate place
In which to conjure up, out of touched memory,
    gifts for our innocent young.

    Over the water, black towers stand
    Trickling thin smoke into the heavens.

A rough-tongued wind licks the innards of ears,
Careers us down the paths of the coffin carriers.

Beyond Cavehill

On Cavehill, that house of fame,
Hoar frost and ice are laid thick,
And upon every flat surface
A son or mother has chiselled
The bare facts and the full name
Of one more departed one -
Bloodless, for he gave his blood,
But full in memory, and remembered,
Thrappled and inhumed here
(Given these icy mouths)
Kept and cried over, until kissed
By the sun's merciful breath.

A Disused Hill Quarry

i

Itinerant tinkers and tinkerers with ideas
Find difficulty with timetables and itineraries
And miss out on meetings; also, there is no longer
Room under hedges, and suitable caves are barred:
Belonging to the public, they are kept oddly safe
And secured. Campsites are well fenced, too:
There is no room to sit down together to discuss
This and that in the heat of an open fire.

ii

This quarry was hewn out a long time ago;
Slabs, jacked off the walls with crowbar, and sweat,
Sledge hammer and iron spike, and a broken back
Or two. The space now left is elegant,
In its way. The gravelled floor smooth, moss-carpeted,
With thin green grass shoots there as for decoration:
A fine amphitheatre to be open only to such prophets,
Their grunting enunciations, their hoarse articulations.

The Sperrins

The glens and valleys are deep-sided and warm
> *In spring the wind is green but yellow specked-and-*
> *flecked*

The black rivers give passage to little fish
> *In autumn the winds are burnished with orange*
> *In winter the wind is white and grey*

The black waters carry gold and tints of bog-earth
> *In summer the wind is green but threaded with yellow*
> *and scarlet*

Only giants can step across Tir-Owen in cold blood

A Hospital on the Outskirts of a Town

After so long on the road we grew tired
And took a short-cut through the shaved grounds
Of a mental institution, passing quickly
A line of people in blue anoraks,
Each clutching a seeming-light little suitcase.
"We are being sent back to the community"
One said, her round face glowing, proud
And radiant and committed to it, she was.
Meanwhile, a man raised up on a small balcony
Spoke, denouncing the word *History*, declaiming,
"There never was a Golden Age, only men and women
Struggling to get a purchase on the great wall of time."
Enumerating with sounds and sketching finger
Specifications of *Climbs*, with their numerous meagre figures;
Some few had, he indicated, *String* or *Thread* tied to the waist
Dangling for those *Few Sighted Ones Coming On* to grasp after.
"They reach up into the past, seeking assistance there," he said,
"If they fail they fall back into the future, alone and lost."

One Face in a Dancehall

The foundation for this wreck of a face was there,
> even then,
Clearly stated in the 'fifties black and white photograph,
> (little contrast, decently composed),
The cheek-bone, forehead, jaw-bone, under taut skin
> fleshless almost, but not quite;
Not an aristocratic face, you are given to understand:
> no real past there
Outing in the keenness, the sharpness, in the contour or
> in the gaze.
This man's eye, established in a flat structured cranium,
> has been whetted to suffer.
There is no question in there, but only because he has never known
> how or why to; or who is who.

A Masked Ball in the Big House

Masked, but with dignity and some presence,
In a corner stood Greed and Exploitation
Dressed in under-stated severity and style -
Good tweeds, well-polished brogues.
Without apology, I removed their masks,
One in each hand, and found, underneath,
The features of Death and Corruption.

We came only because you needed us, haughty
Now, they let it be known before departing.

University Libraries
Coleraine, Jordanstown, Belfast, Londonderry.

Down on the main floor, behind sagging stacks
Beckett and Joyce are engaged in punning
Competitions. The lights are off and Joyce
Hunkers in the dim aisle while the other is inched
Into a corner, his narrow shoulders
Fighting the acute angle's vice.
Like light darts, their constructions fly and die.
In the gallery Swift sniffs in half approval,
Drawn by the pity of their childish skelping play,
His fingers knitted under his own dark blanket.

It is after ten and the place is empty.
Teachers and students do not have pass keys.
The cleaners have wands, they come and they go,
With clanking mop-pail, careless dusting cloths
And all classes of gossip. They make short shift
Of the fine dust that loiters between dry leaves.

Come eleven, all is finished. Goodnight Lou.
Goodnight girls. Goodnight May. Goodnight.
See you the morrow. Goodnight. Goodnight. Goodnight . . .

In the dying fall of the dying day
Egregious egocentrics turn out to play.

Country Towns

i

This is where Europe ends, over the black rocks
    and into the grey sea.
A week spent travelling through country towns,
    each with its entombed streets
Enclaves of hot ministries and cold beds,
    habitat of time's eunuchs
Sucked dry of valour on monochrome Sundays
    where each assembles alone,
Means, between each, arriving at the junction
    where the gardeners work
Beating back the bracken, bramble and thorn,
    Cultivating rights of passage
Along which way your judgement may take you:
    Not spoiled for choice, but making it.

ii

In the anonymous heart of one small town,
Its walled street, greying and rough-plastered,
Like a tunnel rising up out of the west,
A radical entrepreneur has established
A college, or school, of erotic art,
Socks and shoes abandoned in its hallway,
Wooden-pegged walls flagged with careless shifts.

On the hill, a deadening bell irredeemably drums guidance
To the tongues fluttering, like doves above a field of corn.

Graveyards

We could plunder through burial grounds for ever
Making safe stepping stones of the fallen stones
Scraping moss out of each incised line of evidence.
In the autumn of the year in such places
The slightest breath of air sets leaves whispering;
The sap gone out of them now, they are fussy,
They strive to protest in the face of life,
Snapping spitefully before the fact of life.
Children and lovers delight to kick them aside;
In their state, they have no mind for the departed,
They have no bone to pick with sad martyrs.

From Grainan of Aileach to Derry - 21 December ―――

Like champagne, not long opened, the bound stars
Stir under furred ice. Storms are fermenting
Up in the arctic. There's a rawness now
In the air, and word of sleet and snowstorms
Pervades the streets. On the ranked Christmas trees
Lights flash and are gone and in those many
Little interludes hope dies: or say, rather,
That fear is bestirred; and then the lights rekindle.
At its farthest limit the winter sun
Stiffens into a stillness. Time hesitates.
Silence wraps itself about the rage and roar
Of all those last minute gettings and baggings.
All breathing ceases in this stark confrontation
Of all the earth's bright days and all dark nights.

Epilogue

i
At this ford, famously, five townlands meet.
The integrity of these old boundaries
Is beyond question. Any nomadic
Individual who wanders, fancy free,
Here will complicate important issues
(As one spider would, picknicking in another's web)
It's not trespassing, but the act of trespassing
That is taboo: that is something Cuchulainn knew.

ii
Here's where well-regulated hedges and planned fields
Sit squared between the meadows and the uplands;
There the treeline marks where border dispute
Between sapling and mountain grass is settled;
Streams, dikes, ditches, hump and hollow witness ancient realms;
A sprinkle of snow caps still the hill's top;
Bird, beast and man have retired; it is empty, almost.

iii
An old farmer, general to one manoeuvring dog,
Armoured in layered work-clothes and the jacket
Of what must once have been his Sunday suit,
Comes slapping down from the hill with his cattle;
Clods and spray flying they shoulder across.
Bending, he unlocks his cycle and rides after,
The plastic-coated chain left curled where it fell.
Water-drops, like diamonds, hardened in light,
Spew sharply from the silver rims of his wheels;
Travelling into the west, a chariot of fire,
Black and red-rimmed, arrant as any warrior,
His cry of "Hup!", "Hup!", compelling all before.

iv
After the feast of Imbolc, when Spring comes,
Things will get back to normal. Day and night
Will stand distinct again. The ice melted;
The spancel ring cleaned, we shall tongue its words.
The ford waters flowing, shallow and strong;
To that tune we shall learn the proper steps,
Where to cross and how to cross, and when to recross.